FUCHSIAS

KENNETH A. BECKETT

HarperCollins*Publishers*

Products mentioned in this book

Benlate* + 'Activex'	contains	benomyl
'Kerispray'	contains	pirimiphos-methyl
'Picket'	contains	permethrin
ICI Slug Pellets	contains	metaldehyde
'Sybol'	contains	pirimiphos-methyl

Products marked thus '*Sybol*' are trade marks of Imperial Chemical Industries plc
Benlate* is a registered trade mark of Du Pont's
Read the label before you buy: use pesticides safely.

Editor Emma Johnson
Designers James Marks, Steve Wilson
Picture research Moira McIlroy

First published 1988 by
HarperCollins Publishers

This edition published 1992

© Marshall Cavendish Limited 1985, 1988, 1992

A CIP catalogue record for this book is available from the British Library.

Photoset by Bookworm Typesetting
Printed and bound in Hong Kong by Dai Nippon Printing Company

Front cover: Fuchsia 'Voodoo'
Back cover: Fuchsia 'Abbe Farges'
Both photographs by The Harry Smith Horticultural Photographic
Collection

CONTENTS

INTRODUCTION

Slender, elegantly arching growth, neat foliage and dainty colourful, but not shrill-toned, pendent flowers are the hallmarks of the fuchsia. Few plants combine these characteristics so successfully or are so easy to grow, hence their popularity as pot plants for the home and greenhouse and as garden decoration.

Most of the fuchsias we grow today are man-made hybrids with fancy names; they are technically known as cultivars (cultivated varieties) to distinguish them from genuinely wild varieties. Thousands of cultivars have been raised during the past 150 years and it says much for the standards of the early breeders that there are today vintage fuchsias of 100 years old or more rubbing shoulders with the most recently produced ones. The same cannot be said, for example, of chrysanthemums and dahlias. These many fuchsia cultivars are derived from a mere handful of wild species. This is somewhat surprising when one realises how varied this large genus is. About 100 species are known, most of them from Mexico, south to Chile, but there are a few in the West Indies, Tahiti and New Zealand. A wide range of growth form is found, from small carpeters like *F.procumbens* to the tree-sized *F.excorticata*. Most species are shrubs, some evergreen, others deciduous. A few have tubers like a dahlia and some are epiphytic on mossy rocks and trees.

The first fuchsia to be named was *F.triphylla*. It was found on the West Indian Island of San Domingo (Haiti) by Father Charles Plumier (1646-1704), a French Franciscan monk, traveller and botanist. This intrepid missionary had, by 1690, visited several of the West Indian Islands recording the plants he saw with remarkably accurate drawings. He also revived the old custom of naming new plant genera after people, choosing Leonhart Fuchs to perpetuate the fuchsia. Fuchs (1501-66) was a German doctor/herbalist who held the Chair of Medicine at Tubingen University from 1535 to his death in 1566. Apart from *Fuchsia*, he is best remembered today for

his Herbal which is embellished with some excellent woodcut illustrations.

F.triphylla was described in 1703 but not introduced into cultivation for another 180 years. During this time all the familiar species which were to become the parents of our cultivars, were introduced. The years 1788-89 saw *F. coccinea* from Brazil and the similar but much hardier *F.magellanica* from Chile. *F.fulgens* came in 1830, *F.corymbiflora* in 1840, *F.decussata* and *F.denticulata* in 1843-4. Several others were introduced during this time but only the above named have played a primary role as parents of the modern fuchsia cultivars.

At this point it is worthwhile briefly regarding the unique structure of the fuchsia flower. It is divided into fours, not the commonest occurrence among flowers in general; four sepals and petals joined to a bell or trumpet-shaped

tube. This tube arises from an ovoid green ovary (which later became a juicy, edible but insipid black-purple berry). There are eight slender stamens and a long club-tipped style. Unlike most other flowers, the sepals are coloured or white, sometimes with green tips. The tube can also be white or coloured. *Fuchsia procumbens* is the only cultivated species with a yellow tube. Usually the four petals overlap to form a deep bell but in some species and cultivars they are flared out, like a ballet skirt. Their colouring is not very varied but embraces many subtle shades of red, pink, purple and white. Looking at the many popular cultivars it can be seen that some have short tubes, others longer ones. This characteristic above all others gives each cultivar its distinctive appearance, though the length and stance of sepals and flaring of petals all play their part in making each cultivar truly distinct.

Fuchsia triphylla (top left) makes a splendid flowering shrub for frost-free areas. *Fuchsia magellanica*

'Aurea' (top); behind is *Phygelius aequalis*. *Fuchsia magellanica* 'Riccartonii' (above) makes a good hedge.

7

It seems fairly certain that the earliest fuchsia hybrids were made in Britain in the early years of the last century. *F.magellanica* and/or *F.coccinea* were the primary parents and the characters of these two species still shine out in many of the newest cultivars produced today. In 1832 the white-tubed, white-sepalled 'Venus Victrix' arose and though it is most likely simply a mutant of *F.magellanica* and not a purpose-made hybrid, it played a great part in the ancestry of white and near white cultivars. After 1830, *F.fulgens*, with its very long-tubed, red flowers, increasingly played its part in the many hybrids attempted.

By the middle years of last century most of the other familiar fuchsia cultivar characteristics had occurred, namely double, semi-double and semi-erect flowers, variegated and golden foliage. From this era also come several cultivars that are just as valuable in today's greenhouse and garden displays as more recently lauded ones. 'Corallina' was put on the market in 1844 and its low ground-covering habit assures its steady popularity and garden value. Equally hardy, 'Chillerton Beauty' followed in 1847 and the delightful little 'Tom Thumb' in 1850. Then came the white and red, indispensably hardy 'Mme Cornelisson' (1860), the upward-facing flowered 'Bon Accorde' (1861) and the semi-double 'Lena'. Two of the finest foliage cultivars are also of this period, 'Golden Treasure' (1860) and 'Cloth of Gold' (1863).

French and German breeders vied with the British during this period and from then on a flurry of cultivars was released right up to the First World War. From then on

Fuchsia coccinea (above), known for almost 200 years. *Fuchsia magellanica* 'Gracilis versicolor' (right). Raised in 1860, 'Mme Cornelissen' (far right) is still one of the best hardy sorts. 'Tom Thumb' (top right), a first-rate miniature.

there was a decline of interest in Britain and Europe. However, in the late 1920s the baton of interest was taken up by the Americans (in California) and from then on breeders there dominated the fuchsia scene. Happily, the flood of American cultivars rekindled British interest, and, during the last 30 years, breeders here have again played a significant part in furthering the fuchsia's popularity.

Interest in fuchsias is now worldwide where climatic conditions are suitable, as the list of societies and clubs devoted to its culture indicates. America started it off with the National Fuchsia Society (formerly American F.S.) in 1929. Britain followed in 1938, then came New Zealand, Holland, Zimbabwe, Australia, Denmark, France and Germany. There is also much interest in Norway, Romania, Spain, Switzerland and Japan.

USING FUCHSIAS

With its long flowering season, ease of training and natural range of growth forms, the fuchsia can be put to a wide range of uses. Pre-eminent, however, is its value as a pot plant for the greenhouse. It is wonderfully amenable to the constrictions of container culture; splendidly floriferous specimens can be had in only six to nine months from the insertion of small cuttings.

By making a varied selection of species and cultivars, even a large greenhouse can be entirely devoted to fuchsias in a very satisfying way. For less devoted enthusiasts, selected cultivars can be used as points of focal interest among other plants. Alternatively, they can play a lesser role by contrasting or blending with other plants. For example, fuchsias blend particularly well with grey and silver-leaved plants, especially if these are of a feathery nature. Recommended species are: *Tanacetum ptarmiciflorum* (often sold as *Cineraria candicans)* or *Centaurea gymnocarpa (C.cineraria).* Good contrast can be obtained by using a background of larger leaved plants, for example *Acalypha, Begonia rex, Dracaena,* and *Sparmannia.*

As Houseplants Although somewhat less successful than in a greenhouse, fuchsias make good short-term houseplants if sited with care. They need good light, but not the direct rays of summer sun. They also need modicum of humidity to succeed. A well-grown bush fuchsia in full bloom makes a splendid centrepiece for a deep window ledge.

The low dense habit of 'Edinensis' makes it useful as ground cover. 'Pink Dessert' (above) makes a good pot plant for the home.

Fuchsia magellanica 'Gracilis' (below) is the hardiest of all.

In the Garden Soon after the first hybrids were raised, their potential as plants for bedding outside in the summer was realised. This practice continues today, particularly in our public parks. There is no doubt that this is a most effective way of using fuchsias. On the other hand, bedding-out is a labour intensive form of gardening very much less popular than it once was. Of course pot-grown specimens can be planted in a variety of sites around the garden, perhaps to fill in an area of spring bulbs or to brighten up gaps in a shrub or mixed border. This is using fuchsias as half-hardy annuals for a summer or early autumn display, then lifting and returning them indoors or to the greenhouse. There are, of course, hardy fuchsias and these can play a much more permanent role in the garden.

Fuchsia magellanica and its variants is virtually hardy throughout the British Isles, and though often cut back to ground level in bad winters, is seldom killed. Many of the hybrid cultivars raised from it are equally or almost as hardy and make most decorative plants for the garden.

In the coldest areas they make good foundation plants at the foot of a sheltered wall. The taller growing sorts can be trained out flat and are particularly effective in this way. Elsewhere they can be grown in the open, in mixed and shrub borders or in beds on their own. They combine particularly well with some of the smaller evergreen shrubs such as hebe, *Ilex crenata*, *Helichrysum splendidum*, *Senecio* X 'Sunshine' (*S.greyi*), *Cassinia vauvilliersii* and *Berberis candidula*. Finally, if you are looking for long flowering plants for patio and terrace containers, the fuchsia is ideal.

CULTIVATION

Although fairly adaptable plants, fuchsias need certain basic cultural requirements to succeed well. In spring young plants should be nurtured in a reasonably warm, humid atmosphere in the home to stimulate vigorous growth.

In the Home As we have seen already, fuchsias make effective houseplants, but they must be sited with care. Lighting is a major problem. Fuchsias need fairly bright light to stay in a healthy flowering state, but the direct rays of a summer sun shining through a nearby window are usually too hot. As a result, leaf scorch may occur and flower buds may fall before opening. From late spring to early autumn the plants must be either screened with a light net curtain or brought

'Empress of Prussia' (left) has graced our gardens and greenhouses since 1868.
'Brilliant' (above), one of the most richly hued of all fuchsias.
Charming and vigorous, 'Display' (right) has been popular for 100 years.

further into the room, say 90-120cm (3-4ft) away from unscreened glass. Either way, the plants must be turned regularly, otherwise all young growth will grow towards the light and the plants will become lop-sided. Heating is also important, but high temperatures are not required. An ideal maximum day temperature in summer is around 24°C (75°F), though up to 30°C (85°F) is tolerated. It is important

that the temperature drops to about 18°C (65°F) or below at night which it usually does during a British summer. For this reason rooms heated to above this level are not really suitable. For such rooms houseplants of tropical origin are best. If plants are to be kept indoors over the winter period a cool room is best and the plants should be watered sparingly. Some cultivars will even provide flowers if kept at 15-18°C (59-65°F) and given full light.

Fuchsias appreciate a moderately humid atmosphere. In the home the pots are best stood on trays of moist peat or gravel and, during the summer, they can be mist-sprayed with rain or soft water at least once a day.

Watering must be attended to regularly and carried out with care.

More pot plants (and not just fuchsias) have died or been spoilt by over- or under-watering than by any other cause. While they are actively growing, fuchsias must be kept moist but not wet. Over-watering can lead to root rot and rapid deterioration of the plant.

There are various time-honoured ways of telling when the soil in a container is drying out. A reasonably reliable way is to heft a pot of dryish soil, firmed as though for potting. The pot is then thoroughly watered and hefted again. The weight difference is considerable and can be used as a guide when watering. The material of which the container is made is obviously an important factor and clay and plastic pots must be treated separately.

A method favoured by many people, professionals included, is to look at the soil surface. If it is pale or whitish in tone it will be dry or drying. If it is dark it will be damp or even wet. This works well for clay pots, but the compost in plastic containers can look dry on the surface but still be moist enough. Scratching the surface with the finger tip will reveal how moist it is underneath. If the soil feels dry 1cm (¼in) down, water is needed. Rapping the pots with your knuckles or a small tapper (easily made with a small wooden cotton-reel and a slim cane) is another much used method. If a ringing tone is given out, water is needed. If the sound is dull and somewhat hollow the compost is moist to wet. However, this method only really works with clay pots and if the container is cracked it makes a difference to the pitch, so that mistakes can be made. Also, pot-bound and newly potted plants sound different. You must experiment with these methods then stick to the one that seems most successful.

In the Greenhouse If a greenhouse is being constructed with the primary intention of having a fuchsia collection, it should not be less than 2.4 × 1.8m (8 × 6ft). Smaller houses are difficult to prevent from over-heating in summer. If it is intended to keep the fuchsias growing through the winter, the long axis of the greenhouse should be aligned east-west. This will ensure maximum winter light when the sun is low to the south. For this reason, although it is not always possible to site a greenhouse in the best position, it is important to make sure the south aspect is open to the sky in winter. A little east or west shade in summer is permissable.

If bush-trained plants are of primary interest then the greenhouse will need strong benching. This brings the plants nearer to eye-level, and to the light. Standard trained plants need more head room and are stood on the floor as soon as they are 45-60cm (1½-2ft) tall.

To overwinter pot-grown fuchsias, a heat source is necessary. This need be no more than will keep out frost if the plants are to be kept almost dry and dormant. If young plants are to keep growing, or older ones are to provide some flowers, a greater source of warmth is needed. Solid fuel or oil-fired boilers linked to hot water pipes is generally a reliable method, but expensive to instal. Gas and electricity can also be used to heat water, but are best used in a more direct way with special heaters. Most convenient of all is the electric fan heater in conjunction with a thermostat. Although a little more expensive to run than other fuels, it more than makes up for it in convenience. It is, however, advisable to have a simple paraffin heater as a stand-by during power cuts. As far as costing goes it is twice as expensive to maintain a minimum of 13°C (55°F) than it is to keep a temperature of 7°C (45°F). The former temperature will ensure some growth and flowers; the latter will merely keep the plants alive.

Fuchsias dislike a stagnant atmosphere and the greenhouse

must be ventilated once the temperature rises to 10°C (50°F). If it is difficult to keep the temperature down to 24-26°C (75-80°F) with full ventilation, then light shading will be needed. This can be applied in various ways. The best, but also the most expensive, is roller blinds. These can be lowered and raised only when required. Spray-on compounds, even if they rub off easily, are more permanent, and during dull periods the plants can suffer. A compromise is to hang sheets of netting, cotton sheeting or white or green opaque plastic sheets inside the greenhouse between the plants and the glass.

All the comments on watering, made under the houseplant heading above, apply to container plants in the greenhouse. The main thing to realise is that, during warm weather at least, well-rooted pot plants will dry out even more quickly than in the home. Humidity is much more easily provided in a greenhouse by the simple practice known as damping down. Using a can or hose with a rose on the end, thoroughly wet the floor and bench between the pots once a day or even twice during really warm spells.

For the fuchsia enthusiast who is away at work all day most, if not all, of these essential practices can be taken care of automatically. Watering can be done with capillary matting or sand beds kept constantly moist by a piped water supply via a header tank and ballcock valve. Humidity is provided from misting nozzles linked to an electronic-leaf-type switch (as used in mist propagation). There are several devices for raising ventilators when the temperature reaches a certain level. Likewise, roller blinds can be coupled with an electric motor which is in turn linked to a thermostat. Useful though these aids undoubtedly are, They in no way add up to a perfect substitute for the personal touch. Plants to be proud of are never produced by automation.

A well grown standard of 'Blue Lagoon' (top left) 'Gay Fandango' (above), a particularly elegant fuchsia. 'Peppermint Stick' (right).

PROPAGATION

Although fuchsias are shrubs, and relatively long lived when grown as pot plants, the most satisfactory specimens are young ones. This necessitates a certain amount of regular propagation, either annually or biennially. Fuchsia cultivars are increased entirely by stem cuttings which are easy to root with simple equipment. Plants can also be raised from seed, but cultivars do not come true to type and species root so easily from cuttings that seed sowing is seldom worthwhile.

Before cuttings can be taken, some sort of a propagator must be obtained or devised and a rooting medium prepared. Most satisfactory are the custom-made propagators consisting of a plastic tray and a rigid transparent cover. Ideally, one with an electric heating element should be purchased. Alternatively, pots, pans or trays can be placed in a plastic bag. Ribs of stout galvanized wire will prevent the bag from collapsing on top of the cuttings. If early spring cuttings are being taken, heating is necessary. An economic way of providing this is to use soil-warming cables. These are placed on the greenhouse bench, then covered with 2.5cm (1in) of sand. Pots and boxes of cuttings are then stood on the sand, which must be kept damp. A minimum temperature of 18°C (65°F) is required for rapid and sure rooting. Propagators used in the summer to early autumn period must be shaded from direct sunlight; closed plastic and glass-covered propagators can quickly build up lethally high temperatures if placed in direct sun.

Rooting media, into which the cuttings are inserted, can vary greatly, but must be well aerated and free from pest and disease organisms. Highly recommended is a 50/50 mixture of moss peat and coarse sand or fine perlite. Vermiculite can be substituted for the perlite. Sand, perlite or vermiculite can also be used by themselves. Even pure loose peat can be used successfully.

Large quantities of cuttings are best placed in rows in boxes, but smaller amounts can be placed around the edges of pots or pans. Plastic or clay pots are suitable, though clay ones, being porous to air and moisture, are more successful. Cuttings should be inserted about

one third of their stem length. They can be dipped into a rooting hormone powder, such as 'Keriroot' first, but fuchsias root perfectly satisfactorily without this aid. There is no correct distance at which to set cuttings apart, but ideally, the leaves of each one should just overlap those of its neighbour. Leaves transpire water vapour and at this spacing the cuttings help to provide each other with a humid atmosphere. At a wider spacing this situation is less efficient, at at closer one the newly formed roots quickly tangle and can break off when separated for potting. As soon as the cuttings are inserted they should be sprayed with a fungicide, such as Benlate + 'Activex'. This prevents diseases such

BELOW A demonstration of how the different sorts of fuchsia cuttings, illustrated opposite, are inserted.

RIGHT The five basic kinds of fuchsia cuttings, all severed from one current season's stem.

Heel cuttings are not essential for fuchsias, but are an advantage late in the season. Grasp a current season's shoot at its base with thumb and forefinger and pull backwards and downwards (1).

As soon as the shoot is removed from its parent stem, carefully cut away the tail of the heel as this is more likely to root (2). Apply a rooting compound and insert immediately into a rooting medium.

as grey mould from getting a hold.

Given the right conditions practically any piece of fuchsia stem will root and grow. However, experience has shown that the age of the stem and the way it is trimmed effects its subsequent performance. There are three main sorts of cuttings, semi-hardwood, semi-softwood and softwood. Semi-hardwoods are taken from mid to late summer; they are side stems just starting to become woody at the base. These can either be cut off flush with the parent stem or gently pulled off by levering backwards and downwards. This will provide a 'heel' of the parent stem. However, cuttings with heels, though essential for the rooting of some shrub cuttings, are not needed for fuchsias. Cuttings removed flush from the parent stem are cut cleanly beneath the lowest leaf pair or node, then prepared as for heel cuttings. A version of this is known as a basal cutting. It is usually taken with a heel, but is made much shorter, being trimmed above the lowest pair of leaves. The main advantage of the short basal cutting is that it allows the rest of the stem to be used for propagation. The middle section of such a stem provides several kinds of semi-soft cuttings. Pieces with two or three leaf pairs (nodes) can be cut out, slicing cleanly below and above a node. The lowest leaf pair is then removed and the cutting is ready for insertion.

If as many plants as possible are required from a limited amount of propagating material, the stem can be cut into short pieces, each with one leaf pair. These are known as leaf bud or internodal cuttings. The stem is cut just above the leaf pair and 2.5cm (1in) below. For even more plants, each leaf bud cutting can be split longitudinally, so that each cutting has one leaf and a half a stem. Both are inserted up to the base of the leaf stalk. The extreme growing tip provides a softwood cutting. It should have a stem length of at least 2.5cm (1in) with a pair of half-grown leaves. Softwood cuttings can also be taken from late winter to spring. The advantage of this method is that the cuttings root rapidly and grow away without any check. Sizeable plants in full bloom can be had in about six months. Late

1. Fill a seed tray proud of the rim with cuttings compost. Tap to settle, then strike off level.

2. Firm lightly with a wooden presser (a brick can be used as a make-shift alternative).

3. Remove suitable shoots for cuttings from a previously cutback, pest and disease-free plant.

4. Prepare cuttings carefully.

5. Insert in cuttings compost using a dibber, firming gently.

6. Water with a fine-rosed watering can, then place in a propagating frame.

summer cuttings will produce young plants at the onset of winter which will need to be kept ticking over with artificial warmth. Softwood cuttings of this type are taken from well-grown plants of the previous year or older. In the previous late autumn they are kept on the dry side and allowed to become chilled; slight frost will do no harm. From the turn of the year onwards, each plant is spurred back, thoroughly watered and placed in a greenhouse or on a sunny window ledge at not less than 7°C (45°F) and ideally 10°C (50°F). As soon as the young shoots are 2.5cm (1in) long they are severed close to their point of origin with a razor blade or very sharp knife and inserted immediately up to the lowest leaf pair.

Signs of rooting can be seen in a general perking up of all the leaves and new growth beginning, either from the top or from the leaf axils. At this point the cuttings are turned out carefully and placed singly in 6-7.5cm (2½-3in) of a growing compost.

CONTAINERS AND POTTING

The best container-grown fuchsia plants are those that are allowed to grow vigorously from the time the rooted cutting is potted until it is in full bloom. For this, each plant must have a steady supply of nutrients such as only a properly formulated potting compost can provide.

In the garden the roots of a plant spread far and wide in search of food and moisture. In a pot they are crammed into a very much smaller volume of soil. Therefore, garden soil alone is not a suitable rooting medium unless enriched with fertiliser or regularly supplied with extra plant food in liquid form.

Until recent times, gardeners mixed up their own potting composts, using turfy loam or garden soil mixed with decayed manure and/or leafmould, plus a little coarse sand. Such mixes can produce excellent results, but beware of soil pests, diseases and weeds. Nowadays there are many scientifically formulated composts and it is recommended that the beginner uses them. If reliably made the John Innes potting composts are excellent for fuchsias. Unfortunately the John Innes formula was not patented and sub-standard versions are on the market. All the so-called soil-less potting mixes, such as 'Kericompost', are good, but plants growing in them must be given regular liquid food such as ICI Liquid Growmore once the containers are filled with roots.

Containers To grow a collection of fuchsia plants from cuttings to maturity, a range of flowerpot sizes will be required. The most useful sizes are 7.5cm (3in), 13cm (5in), 15cm (6in) and 18cm (7in). Plastic pots are now used by most gardeners and are excellent for fuchsias. Nevertheless, the well aerated nature of a clay pot can ensure a superb specimen plant, everything else being equal.

Potting Whatever the plant it must be potted with care. This is especially important when the rooted fuch-

1. When rooted and just starting to grow, lift carefully with a strong label or widger.

2. Place some potting soil in the pot, lower the cutting so that its roots rest on it, then fill around with more.

3. Press firmly, but gently, with the finger tips, then tap the pot to settle the surface. Water with a fine-rosed watering can.

sia cutting goes into its first container. A little compost is placed in the bottom of a 7.5cm (3in) pot and the rooted cutting is lowered onto this. More compost is filled in around it and the container is tapped to settle the cutting around the roots. Next, the soil is firmed with the finger tips. Soil-less composts should be firmed more lightly than loam-based ones. Drainage crocks are not needed in pot sizes up to 15cm (6in) in diameter.

Once the plant is growing well and the roots start to mesh on the surface of the soil ball, it is time for it to be potted-on into a larger container – usually a 13cm (5in) one. Once again soil is placed in the bottom, just enough to allow adequate room for watering when the plant root-ball is lowered in. (A gap about one-seventh of the pot depth should be left for this). Soil is filled in around the root-ball and firmed, then totted up and firmed again.

When roots again start to mesh on the root-ball, the plant must be potted on once more. Usually this next potting is the final one and into a 15cm (6in) or 18cm (7in) container. Only standards, pyramids, conicals and other large trained specimens will need bigger containers.

BELOW 'Avon Gem', a good British fuchsia of recent vintage.

BOTTOM 'Margaret Roe' forms an erect, free-blooming bush.

RE-POTTING AND WINTER CARE

Once a fuchsia plant is established in its final pot and has grown to full size, it can only be maintained in this state by feeding, top-dressing and re-potting. A recommended sequence of events is to re-pot the plants each other year and to top-dress them the years in between. Regular feeding, mainly in liquid form, is needed throughout the growing season.

Re-potting The action of re-potting a plant differs from potting-on, though the term is often loosely used for both practices. Potting-on always implies moving on into a larger container, re-potting is a way of maintaining a plant in the same sized pot. Re-potting is carried out when the plant is dormant or almost so, usually after pruning in late winter or early spring. First it is turned out of its pot, then the root ball is reduced all over by about a quarter. This can be done easily with the points of a small fork. A useful tool can be made from an old kitchen fork by bending the end 6mm (¼in) of the prongs over at right angles. This will quickly strip off a layer of soil, and some of the fine roots down to the required depth. Once this is done, the plant is returned to its pot, or another of the same size, and dealt with as for potting-on. If the soil seems dry, the root ball should be soaked first.

Top-dressing Less drastic than re-potting, top-dressing is a similar kind of operation, but only the top of the root ball is removed. The plant is left in its pot and a small hand fork is used to reduce soil and roots equal to one fifth to one quarter of the root ball depth. The modified kitchen fork mentioned above is even more efficient. The gap is filled with a rich compost, such as the peat-based 'Kericompost', and pressed firm.

After re-potting and top-dressing, the plants must be watered and if possible kept a little warmer to

1. Strip a layer of soil and fine roots down to ⅕ of total root ball depth.

2. Replace the stripped off soil with fresh potting compost.

3. Firm the new compost, then tap the pot to settle the surface. Water with a fine-rosed can.

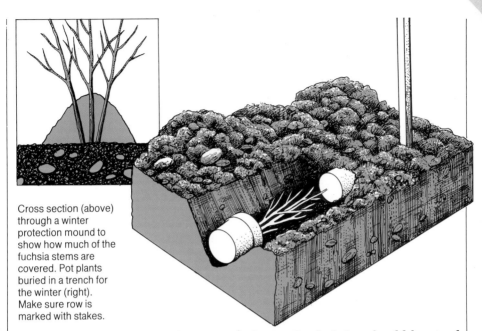

Cross section (above) through a winter protection mound to show how much of the fuchsia stems are covered. Pot plants buried in a trench for the winter (right). Make sure row is marked with stakes.

encourage growth. If the plants are grown without artificial heat, these operations are best delayed until the warmer weather of spring.

Feeding Re-potting and top-dressing will not maintain a fuchsia plant in a healthy free-blooming state for the whole of a growing season and supplementary feeding is essential. Highly recommended are the various proprietary liquid feeds, such as ICI Liquid Growmore. These should be applied according to makers' instructions, ideally little and often, rather than large doses at longer intervals. They should be started about six weeks after repotting or when the first flower buds start to show.

Winter Care Mature fuchsia plants of one or more years respond to a resting period. Feeding should cease in early October and as flowering ceases the ventilators should be kept open and heating turned off. If this is not possible, because of other plants, the fuchsias should be stood outside in a sheltered place. Water must be given sparingly and from late October or early November onwards the plants can be kept almost dry. Lie the plants on their sides to prevent rain from soaking them. Light air frost will do no harm, but if colder conditions are forecast the plants must be protected. Sheets of heavy gauge plastic sheeting are suitable for this. Alternatively, they can be brought back into the greenhouse where they will need artificial heat. If heating is not used, the plants must be protected in other ways. The pots can be plunged in soil, mounded around with peat or sand or lagged with bracken or sacking. During prolonged cold spells the tops must be covered as well. The degree of protection given entirely depends on the severity of the winter; in cold areas the plants can be pruned then completely buried 15cm (6in) deep, lying on their sides. The soil must of course be light and free-draining.

PLANT FORM AND TRAINING

Allowed to grow naturally, most fuchsias form spreading or rounded bushes. Their speed of growth, however, and ability to produce an abundance of side shoots when pruned, makes them ideal subjects for training into a variety of forms. The ones most popular with growers are shrub, bush, ball, standard, pillar and pyramid, plus the more tricky espalier and fan. All trained forms must be started soon after the rooted cuttings are established in their first pots.

Shrub This is the easiest form of training. The tip of the young plant is pinched out at three leaf pairs and the subsequent shoots are similarly dealt with. Thereafter, the severity of pinching is optional, but generally shoots are allowed to reach 10-13cm (4-5in) before pinching. All basal shoots and those from below ground level are allowed to develop and fill out the plant structure. Once a suitable framework has been built up, the plant is left to grow and flower. From the time of the last pinching to flowering is six to eight weeks.

Bush Basically this is the same as shrub from a pinching point of view. However, all basal growth is removed and a short leg of not more than 4cm (1½in) between the soil level and first branch is maintained.

Ball The basic training is as for shrub, but only cultivars of arching habit are selected. As the plant builds up, the lower branches are encouraged to arch over the sides of the pot. A well grown ball should cover most of the container.

Standard Basically this is a bush on a leg which can be of variable length. Young plants are kept growing vigorously by regular feeding and keeping all side shoots pinched out. Full standards must have an unbranched stem or leg of not less than 75cm (2½ft) and not more than 1.1m (3½ft). Once the desired height range is reached, the stem is allowed to produce two or three pairs of leaves, then pinched out. Shoots from these topmost leaf axils will form the head of the standard and

bush   ball   pyramid   standard

single

semi-double

double

clustered

Wild fuchsia flowers have four sepals, four petals and eight stamens. Cultivated varieties with this basic form are known as single-flowered. In double-flowered cultivars most of the stamens are transformed into extra petals, giving them a very full appearance. Semi-double blooms have only a few extra petals. Most cultivated fuchsias have one — rarely two or three — flowers in each leaf axil. There is also a small group of species and cultivars which bears flowers in terminal clusters. Typical examples are *F. triphylla* 'Thalia'.

pinching-out is then as for shrub. A cane support a little longer than the desired leg length is needed. Half-standards have a leg length of not less than 45cm (1½ft) and not more than 75cm (2½ft). Quarter standards must have a leg length of between 30cm (1ft) and 45cm (1½ft).

Pyramid A little more care is needed to train a shapely pyramid. There is no height limit, but 90-120cm (3-4ft) is average. A cane support is needed from the first. Young plants are allowed to grow to 23cm (9in) and the top is pinched out. The shoots that develop are allowed to grow three or four pairs of leaves. The strongest of the topmost or leading pair of shoots is then retained, the weaker one removed and all others are pinched out at four or five leaf pairs. When the leading shoot is 23cm (9in) its tip is removed and the process is repeated. The main problem is getting the tiers of branches that form after each pinching of the leading shoot, to continue growing vigorously. Sometimes it is necessary to cut the leading shoot back to its lowest leaf pair to put extra sap flow into the lower side stems. Sometimes lying the plant on its side for a week or so will help by diverting sap flow from the leading to the lateral stems.

PRUNING

Left to themselves and protected from severe frost, most fuchsia cultivars and many species will grow large. Eventually they become straggly and flower less freely. To get the best from a fuchsia plant, whether in a pot in a greenhouse or outside in the garden, it needs pruning. The initial pruning, generally known as pinching or pinching-out, has been mentioned frequently in the training section. It quite literally means pinching the shoot tip between thumb and forefinger and using the nails as scissors to sever the soft young stem. The tissue quickly heals in the region of active growth.

Older stems that have become woody must be cut with clean, sharp secateurs or a pruning knife. It is recommended that the beginner use secateurs as a sharp pruning or budding knife needs some skill to wield efficiently. During the training period pinching should be all that is needed. Occasionally however, a larger stem, partly or fully woody, may look out of place or several may be crowded together and need thinning. The cut is made just above a leaf pair, making sure not to leave a length of stem known as a snag. This can rot and in doing so cause the living stem beneath to die back. In a serious case a whole branchlet could die and spoil the shape of the plant.

The most important secateur pruning comes annually when plants which are being kept for more than one year are severely cut back.

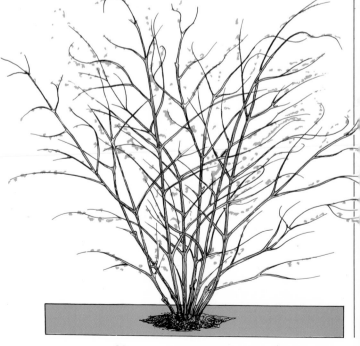

RIGHT Hardy fuchsia stems generally die part of the way back each winter and need to be hard pruned in late spring. The aim is to leave a cluster of strong stem bases from which new growth will arise.

This takes place when the plants are dormant, ideally just before they are started into growth, although it can be done at an earlier stage if this is convenient.

The beginner must first look at his plant carefully, especially if it is a specimen of one year old or less, trained the previous spring and summer. The original stem of the cutting will now be the main axis of the shrub, ball or bush. The tip of the leg of the standard will serve the same function. The branches from this axis are known as laterals. These form the framework of the whole plant, or the head of the standard. The branches from the laterals are known as sub-laterals. In turn, the sub-laterals will bear further branches. The stems to prune are the sub-laterals. Each one is cut back to a stub about 2.5cm (1in) long, and severed it cleanly at the node. The node is the point where the leaves were borne and it carries two tiny buds ready to break into growth the following season. If the young plant has only a minimum of four laterals, the sub-laterals can be left longer so that there are more buds to form more stems and thus make a shapely plant more quickly.

Plants of two or more years old are usually somewhat easier to deal with. Each stem which arose from the sub-laterals the previous season is cut back to a stub carrying one or more nodes. As before, the length of this stub depends on the number of basic branches (original laterals). A certain amount of judgement is needed as a plant gets older, to decide how much to cut out. Younger stems may arise directly from the original laterals, and these can be retained to make a more shapely framework. Old growth can then be removed to make room for them.

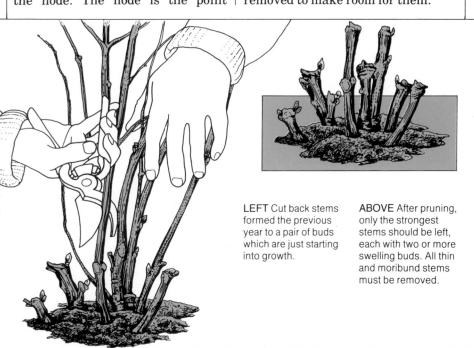

LEFT Cut back stems formed the previous year to a pair of buds which are just starting into growth.

ABOVE After pruning, only the strongest stems should be left, each with two or more swelling buds. All thin and moribund stems must be removed.

FUCHSIAS AS GARDEN PLANTS

For well over 100 years some fuchsias have graced our beds and borders as permanent garden plants. Most frequently planted and by far the hardiest is the Chilean species *F.magellanica*, its varieties and cultivars, but especially *F.m.gracilis* and *molinae*.

Probably all the modern hybrid cultivars we grow have a large part of *magellanica* in their parentage and mainly owing to this a surprisingly high percentage are reasonably hardy, surviving all but the worst winters outside. In addition, some breeders have purposefully set out to produce hardy cultivars. A pioneer in this field was the British enthusiast W.P.Wood, author of the classic *A Fuchsia Survey* (1950). Some of his cultivars of the 1940s are still popular as garden plants.

Soils Fuchsias will grow in a wide variety of soils including acid and chalky ones. The primary consideration is that it should be well drained. Having said that, fuchsias will grow in clay soils, but they die off more readily in winter, probably due to waterlogging and rotting at the roots as much as to cold. Clay soils can be made more amenable with the liberal addition of coarse sand or grit, organic matter such as peat, and well-rotted garden compost or manure. Organic matter contains humus, an essential colloidal substance of fertile soils. Humus coats each soil particle and thus opens it up to air, facilitating the downward flow of water. It also holds a certain amount of water and dissolved plant food, so it is also of great use in improving the light sandy and chalky soils. Organic matter is very much the key to all soil fertility.

A reliable, hardy species, *Fuchsia magellanica* 'Gracilis' (above). 'Princess Dollar' (right), a fine double.

Site Soil conditions, then, are seldom a limiting factor in growing fuchsias outside, but siting can be. For a good floral display at least some sunshine is needed. Full day sun is not necessry, but a site with either morning or afternoon sun is essential. An alternative is a site with both some morning and some afternoon sun (4-6 hours in all is adequate), for example in beds beneath high tree cover or frontal gaps in a shrub border.

Except in the milder coastal areas, particularly in the south and west, fuchsias appreciate a sheltered position. Wind is tolerated but gales can easily break the somewhat brittle branches. In cold areas where winter frosts are known to be more prolonged than elsewhere (mainly north east England, but elsewhere in the north at higher elevations), protected sites are necessary. Beds at the foot of walls, fences and thick hedges are ideal.

Planting Young growth and foliage of all fuchsias is prone to frost damage. For this reason, young plants to be grown outside should not be planted out until late spring or early summer when fear of severe frost has passed. Just prior to planting, a light dressing of general fertiliser should be applied to each planting site and worked in with a hand fork. Growmore at the equivalent of 60-90g (2-3oz) per sq.m (yd) depending on basic soil fertility, is recommended. The plants should be set deeper in the soil than they are in the container, so that stem bases are covered with about 4cm (1½in) of soil. This ensures that when the tops are cut back by frost, buds protected by a soil layer will quickly renew growth in the next season.

Maintenance Except in the mildest areas, most of the top growth of a fuchsia plant will be killed back. The extent to which this happens depends on the severity of the winter. Dead growth must be pruned away. It is best to wait until growth buds are visible in late spring, then to cut back to them, making a clean cut with no snags (see Pruning section). After pruning, a light dressing of fertilizer is recommended, though it is not essential. At the same time a mulch of organic matter will be beneficial, every other spring.

In cold areas, or if a bad winter looks like continuing, the stem bases can be protected by earthing up (as for potatoes) or mounding around with coarse sand or dryish peat covered with plastic sheeting.

Fuchsia magellanica 'Molinae' (above) is often listed under its former name 'Alba'. It is equally as hardy as *F.m.* 'Gracilis' and can make a big bush in a sheltered place.

PESTS AND DISEASES

Like many other popular plant groups, fuchsias are prone to the attack of pests. Fortunately there are not many of importance and most are controllable. Plants under glass are the most susceptible and it is important to keep the greenhouse clean with an annual scrub and wash down with a strong disinfectant.

Be particularly careful with purchased or gift plants; these can harbour just one or two red spider mites or whiteflies which quickly multiply in summer and soon become a major nuisance. Always use insecticides and fungicides according to makers' instructions; too strong a concentrtion can damage the plant as well as killing the pest or disease, too weak a solution is unlikely to be effective.

SYMPTOMS AND TREATMENTS

Leaves deformed Slightly or severely deformed leaves are usually the result of damage by aphids (greenfly and blackfly etc). These tiny, soft-bodied insects usually occur in dense colonies and they suck the sap. Leaves which look tattered and have irregular holes are attacked by one of the species of capsid bug. These are like larger, more flattened aphids, but they are solitary, fast moving and secretive. Spray both pests with 'Sybol', 'Picket' or 'Kerispray'

Leaves dying and with a fluffy, greyish mould See under Stems Wilting.

Leaves with spittle-like masses Outdoor fuchsias are sometimes attacked by the grub (nymph) of the bug known as a froghopper. It sucks the sap and can cause distortion. Both nymphs and froth can be washed off with a forceful jet of

Aphids

Froghopper

water. Spraying with 'Sybol' or 'Kerispray' eradicates this pest.

Leaves with minute, white flies See next entry.

Leaves mottled and/or yellowing Many plants under glass show this symptom, which is caused by red spider mites and whiteflies. Both suck the sap and in severe attacks cause premature leaf-fall. The red or red-spotted mites are almost too small to see, but the whiteflies are readily seen as white flecks when the plant is tapped. 'Sybol' or 'Kerispray' can be used very effectively against both pests.

Leaves eaten Plants inside and outside often have pieces eaten out of the leaves. This denotes the feeding of caterpillars and earwigs, less commonly of slugs and snails. The latter pests leave silvery slime trails so their damage is easily recognised. A spraying with 'Sybol, 'Picket' or malathion kills caterpillars and earwigs. Slugs and snails must be baited with slug pellets containing

metaldehyde or methiocarb. If the damage is slight, it is always worthwhile picking them off by hand.

Stems wilting or dying back The wilting of young stem tips, and sometimes the lower leaves, often denotes the soil-borne fusarium and verticillium diseases. The main diagnostic character is a brown or blackish discolouration in the stem when it is cut through. Treatment is not easy and severely infected plants should be destroyed. Drenching the soil with spray strength Benlate + 'Activex' at 14-day intervals is worth trying. In winter when plants are kept growing with minimal heat, wilting or dying back is accompanied by zones of brown decaying tissue and a fluffy grey-white mould. This is grey mould disease which attacks dying leaves or stems, then works into living tissue. It is worst in still, cool, damp conditions. Raising the temperature and/or giving more ventilation will reduce its incidence. Stems that have been attacked must be cut out and the plant sprayed with Benlate + 'Activex'.

Earwigs

Grey mould

FUCHSIA BREEDING

Producing new varieties of a favourite plant can be a fascinating and all absorbing pastime. It is not restricted to professional plant breeders and anyone with the incentive can have a go. Even if fuchsia breeding is thought of as only a bit of fun, there should be a definite objective in view. For example, it would be nice to have a wider range of flower colour combinations and forms in the low, arching cultivars so useful for hanging baskets.

The would-be breeder must become familiar with all the cultivars that are likely to make suitable parents. This is essential, so that when the seedlings bloom, a good new one will be recognised for what it is right away. Lack of familiarity may mean that a seedling is selected that is no better, or only as good as an existing cultivar. You need to know a little about the structure of a flower and this is shown below. The stamens are composed of a long stalk and a fused pair of oblong lobes. These contain the pollen, the male element of a flower. The ovary contains ovules, each one of which be-

comes a seed when fertilized by a male cell. From the top of the ovary grows a stalk-like style, capped by a club-shaped stigma. Pollen is rubbed off onto the stigma when a bee or other insect is visiting a flower for nectar or pollen gathering. The pollen germinates and a tube grows down the style into an ovary and up to an ovule. A male cell from the pollen grain which has travelled in the tip of the tube, fuses with the ovule and a seed forms.

To pollinate a flower artificially, a bud just cracking open is selected, opened carefully and the anthers snipped off. When the flower opens

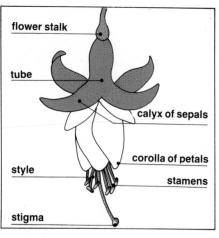

ABOVE Every would-be fuchsia breeder should be familiar with the parts that make up the flower.

'Chequerboard' (right); 'Amy Lye' (far right); 'Rose Churchill' (extreme right).

properly, pollen is taken from the selected male parent and dusted on the stigma. A small brush can be used, or a stamen can be taken with a pair of forceps and used directly on the stigma. It is important that a record is kept, and the pollinated flower must be tagged with the date and both parent names. When the berry ripens, usually turning dark purple, the seed is extracted, either by squashing into a drop of water or directly onto absorbent paper. When dry, the seed is packeted and kept cool and dry until the spring.

The seed is sown thinly and barely covered, using a reliable proprietary seed-sowing compost. For good germination, a temperature of not less than 16°C (60°F) is needed. As soon as the seedlings are up they must be kept in good light so that they develop sturdily. When the first true leaves are seen the seedlings must be pricked off into pans or boxes of potting compost. They should be spaced at about 4cm (1½in) apart each way. Every seedling should be kept, even the tiny ones because sometimes these produce the most interesting results. When the leaves of the young plants start to overlap they must be placed singly in 7.5-9cm (3-3½in) pots. When the plants are well grown they can be hardened off, then planted outside in rows to flower. Alternatively, they can be flowered in 13cm (5in) containers. Devise an efficient system of labelling so that plants of different crosses don't get mixed up.

When the plants flower they must be looked at very critically. If they do not combine the characters they were bred for, or are no better than existing cultivars, they should be discarded. (This can be difficult for the beginner to whom all geese will look like swans). If something good turns up it can be propagated from cuttings for one or two seasons to make sure it grows well, and it can then be shown at one of the meetings held by The British Fuchsia Society. If it really is good a commercial grower will turn up with an offer.

SIXTY OF THE BEST

Several hundreds of distinct fuchsias are commercially available, so deciding what to grow is a matter of personal choice. Those fuchsias described and illustrated here are easily grown, very reliable in their long season of flowering and available from fuchsia specialists and garden centres up and down the country. The catalogues of most fuchsia growers give the date of introduction (when known) and a description.

Aintree

Alice Hoffman

Amy Lye

AINTREE

This single-flowered cultivar has an ivory tube and sepals, slightly pink suffused, and a vivid rose corolla with a hint of purple. The growth habit is erect but also bushy, very suitable for both pot culture and summer bedding.

ALICE HOFFMAN (1911)

Raised in Germany, this hardy cultivar is still one of the best garden fuchsias. Although small, the single flowers are profusely borne over a long season. The tube and sepals are pink and the white corolla has rose veining. Naturally dwarf and erect, it branches freely without pinching.

AMY LYE (1885)

Now a centenarian, this single is one of the early British cultivars almost certainly derived from *F.fulgens*. It has a greenish-white tube, white and green-tipped sepals and a coral-orange corolla. It is almost hardy.

AVON GEM (1978)

This attractive British fuchsia has red tube and sepals and a purple corolla, shading to magenta. It is a vigorous grower, very free-flowering and makes a fine standard. It is best under glass.

BEACON (1871)

A real vintage cultivar, it has single flowers with scarlet tube and sepals and a bright magenta-pink corolla. It has a very compact, erect habit and a long season of flowering. The foliage is large and dark green, making a good foil for the blooms. It is excellent for pots and as a garden plant.

36

BILLY GREEN
The long tube of this fuchsia comes from the first known species, *F.triphylla*, but the colouring of the single blooms is entirely pinkish-salmon. It has an erect habit and is vigorous and bushy.

BLUE WAVES (1954)
This fine double cultivar has poppy-red tube and sepals and a violet-blue corolla. The flowers are large and freely produced on a vigorous, erect plant. In a sheltered spot it makes a fine garden plant.

Blue Waves

BRIGADOON (1957)
Rather willowy in its growth habit, this double cultivar has large flowers from long buds. The sepals are pink with a crepe texture within and the corolla is violet-blue, marbled near the base with pink. Fairly hardy but not usually too successful outside.

Brilliant

BRILLIANT (1865)
This fine old vintage single to semi-double was raised in Britain. It is very vigorous, producing strong arching stems and fairly long-tubed flowers. Tube and sepals are scarlet, the corolla violet-purple veined red. It is useful as a greenhouse and bedding plant and will grow outside in sheltered places.

CALEDONIA (1899)
Raised in France, this hardy fuchsia has the grace and elegance inherent in its wild parent *F.magellanica gracilis*. The small slender, single flowers are freely borne. They have red tubes and sepals and reddish-violet corollas.

Billy Green

CARA MIA (1957)

The long graceful flower of this single cultivar has pale rose-pink tube and sepals and a crimson corolla. They are of good size and produced in profusion.

CASCADE (1937)

Most aptly named, this fine American cultivar has a trailing growth habit which makes it an ideal candidate for a hanging basket. The growth is also very vigorous and can be trained erect to make a weeping standard. Each flower has white tube and sepals, tinted carmine and the corolla is rich carmine.

Chang

Constellation

CHANG (1946)

This colourful American cultivar has great vigour and must be regularly pinched if not required too tall. Each small single flower has a slightly inflated orange-red tube, paler orange sepals with green tips and a bright orange-red corolla. Though best in the greenhouse it can be grown outside in sheltered areas.

CHECKERBOARD (1948)

The very distinctive star-like flower of this cultivar has a red tube, red-base, white slender-pointed sepals and a red corolla. It makes a most decorative free-blooming pot plant.

COCCINEA

Although sometimes confused with *F.magellanica*, this Brazilian species was almost certainly the first fuchsia ever to be cultivated in the British Isles. It is a bushy shrub that grows to about 90cm (3ft) tall. The smallish blooms have red tubes and sepals and violet to purple corollas. Though pleasing, it is less hardy than *F.magellanica* and though of historical interest it is now seldom grown.

CONSTELLATION (1957)

This fine American double has a basically all-white bloom, though the tube is striped and the sepals tipped with green. The bush is sturdy and erect.

DANISH PASTRY

Forming a wide-spreading, almost trailing bush, this attractive fuchsia makes a fine hanging basket specimen. The single flowers have tubes and sepals of palest coral pink and lavender to salmon corollas. They look their best against a background of bright green foliage.

DISPLAY (1881)
This excellent vintage fuchsia has quite a modern look with its short, deep rose-pink tube and sepals, and beautifully flared cerise-pink corolla. It remains today among the best of single cultivars. The plant is short jointed and free-blooming, making a fine bedding and pot plant.

DOCTOR FOSTER (1899)
Although not particularly outstanding when grown among the finer pot specimens, it is a good hardy plant for the garden. The single flowers have scarlet tubes and sepals, and violet-purple corollas.

ETERNAL FLAME (1971)
Comparatively recent as cultivars go, this intriguing fuchsia has salmon-orange sepals and a smoky-rose corolla, streaked or flamed with salmon-red. The flowers are semi-double and freely produced.

FALLING STARS (1941)
Although raised in California, this pleasing fuchsia is usually hardy when grown outside here. It is vigorous, but has a lax habit and needs plenty of pinching back to get a bushy head. Its freely produced single flowers have pink tubes, reddish-pink and salmon sepals and dusky reddish-orange corollas.

EMPRESS OF PRUSSIA (1868)
Despite its age, this is still one of the best large flowered hardy cultivars in its colour range. Each single flower has a bright red tube and sepals and a magenta-red corolla.

GAY FANDANGO (1951)
This excellent all round fuchsia can be trailed in any form and produces its large semi-double flowers freely. Each one has a carmine tube and sepals and a magenta corolla.

Display

Dr Foster

Eternal Flame

GOLDEN MARINKA (1959)

The long-tubed flowers of this highly decorative cultivar are red throughout, though the corolla is a little darker. They contrast delightfully with the yellow and cream variegated leaves. Of trailing habit, both 'Golden Marinka' and its green-leaved progenitor 'Marinka' make superb hanging basket plants.

Golden Lena

Golden Marinka

GOLDEN LENA

This is a variegated-leaved form of the vintage cultivar 'Lena' (1862). Good for pots and outside, it has longish semi-double flowers with flesh-pink tubes and sepals and rosy-purple corollas. It can be grown in any form and makes a good garden plant.

Heidi Weiss

HEIDI WEISS

Upright and compact in habit, this fuchsia has double flowers with cerise-crimson tubes and sepals, and white, scarlet veined corollas. It makes a good pot plant.

Howlett's Hardy

HOWLETT'S HARDY (1952)
Suitable for all kinds of training and good in pots inside or on the patio, this cultivar is pre-eminent as a hardy garden plant. Its single flowers are large, each one with a scarlet tube and sepals and a violet-purple corolla bearing scarlet veins.

INVASION
This is a fine full double, each long-stalked flower having a red tube, broad upswept red sepals and a red-purple corolla. It makes an eye-catching pot plant.

Invasion

KING'S RANSOM (1954)
Clear white tube and green-tipped sepals and a double imperial purple corolla is the hallmark of this striking cultivar. Sturdy and upright in habit, it makes a good pot plant of show class.

LADY THUMB
This is a mutant (sport) of the well known dwarf 'Tom Thumb' (q.v.), but with semi-double flowers with light carmine sepals and a white corolla veined with carmine.

LOVELINESS (1869)
As strikingly attractive now as it must have been when it first bloomed in James Lye's nursery, this vintage cultivar has a long, pure white tube and sepals and a single rosy-cerise corolla. Free-flowering, upright and bushy, it makes a fine pot plant and can be grown outside in sheltered sites.

King's Ransom

Loveliness

MAGELLANICA

This is the hardiest and best known of the species fuchsias and is invariably grown as a garden shrub. In the milder areas it reaches 1.5m (5ft) or more, but elsewhere it is cut back in hard winters. Profusely borne, the small flowers have red tubes and sepals and purple corollas. there are several varieties and cultivars. *F.m.* 'Aurea' has leaves suffused with gold. *F.m.* 'Gracilis' has a more graceful habit, with wand-like stems, narrower leaves and slender flowers of great elegance. 'Gracilis Variegata' has green leaves with creamy-yellow, pink-flushed margins. It is a striking plant even when not in bloom, but a little less hardy than the green-leaved type. 'Gracilis Versicolor' has delightful grey-green foliage which is pink-tinted when young. *F.m molinae*, formerly known as *F.m* 'Alba', is distinguished by its white flowers with a faint flush of mauve. It is the hardiest of all the *magellanica* varieties and cultivars. *F.m* 'Riccartonii' is the most vigorous and the tallest of the magellanica varieties and cultivars. It has slightly larger flowers with richer red sepals and broader petals. This is the tall hedging fuchsia seen in western Ireland and other mild areas.

MARGARET (1943)

One of the best hardy fuchsias produced by W.P.Wood, 'Margaret' makes an upright bushy plant clad with good foliage. In fertile soil it can make a large specimen even in one growing season. The double flowers have carmine tubes and sepals and purple-pink corollas with cerise veining.

Magellanica 'Riccartonii'

Magellanica 'Versicolour'

Mrs Popple

MARGARET ROE (1971)

The single flowers of this charming cultivar have short, wide, rosy-red tubes, sepals of the same colour and pale violet-purple corollas. They are freely produced on erect, bushy plants, and make good pot plants.

MARY (1905)

Produced in Germany by Benstedt, who raised several fine *F.triphylla* hybrids, this cultivar still ranks high as an eye-catching pot plant. The long-tubed flowers are rich scarlet throughout and are carried in trusses typical of *F.triphylla*.

MME CORNELISSEN (1860)

One of the most popular and reliable of the hardy fuchsias, this cultivar can hold its own with anything similar which has been produced since. The single flowers have red tubes and sepals and white corollas with red veins.

MRS POPPLE (1889)

Largely derived from *F.magellanica*, this reliable, attractive hardy cultivar can also be trained in a variety of forms as a pot plant. Its normal habit is upright and bushy with single blooms having cerise-red tubes and sepals and a purple corolla with cerise veins.

MRS LOVELL SWISHER

This fuchsia has fairly long pink tubes and pink sepals and double pink to rose-red corollas. Though elegantly formed, the freely produced flowers are on the small side. It forms a vigorous bush.

ORANGE CRUSH (1972)

Aptly named, this fairly recent cultivar has single flowers in shades of orange; salmon-orange tubes and sepals, and a bright orange corolla. The bush is erect and short-jointed and makes a satisfactory pot plant.

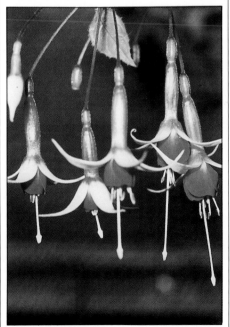

Mrs Lovell Swisher

Orange Crush

PEPPERMINT STICK (1951)

Essentially a greenhouse plant, this fine American double is strong growing and has good foliage. The large flowers have carmine tubes and sepals and a very full corolla, each petal of which is rich purple edged with carmine, creating a striped effect.

PINK DESSERT (1963)

This pretty fuchsia has single self pink flowers, though the corolla is a little darker than the sepals. The flowers have an elegant length and dangle freely from an erect bush.

PINK GALORE (1958)

The tube and sepals of this double cultivar are deep pink, the corolla is candy pink, making it one of the nicest all-pink fuchsias. The growth habit is naturally lax and cascading and ideal for hanging baskets.

PRINCESS DOLLAR (1912)

As vigorous now as it was when it was first raised, this fine old double fuchsia makes a good pot plant and is hardy enough to be grown outside. Each full bloom has a cerise-red tube and sepals and a rich purple corolla, shading to red at the base.

Pink Dessert

Pink Galore

Rose of Castille

ROSE CHURCHILL
This all-pink double fuchsia is a sport from 'Winston Churchill' (1942), a fine full double pink tube and sepals and a blue, pink-splashed and veined corolla. Both cultivars make sturdy bushes and bloom freely. In sheltered sites they can be grown in the garden.

ROSE OF CASTILLE (1869)
Undoubtedly this is one of the classic vintage fuchsias, still very much in demand despite modern competition. Of upright bushy growth it has smallish, profusely borne flowers each with a faintly pink flushed white tube and sepals and a purple, white based corolla. It is equally good as a pot plant or as a garden plant.

ROYAL VELVET (1962)
This is perhaps one of the finest doubles to be raised during the past 20 years. The extra large flowers have red tubes and sepals and a rich royal purple corolla. They are carried freely on erect bushy growth.

Royal Velvet

RUFUS THE RED (1951)
An elegantly formed single flower, entirely of Turkey-red and freely produced, is the hallmark of this attractive cultivar. The plant is erect and bushy and blooms very profusely. It can be grown as a garden plant.

SOUTHGATE
Of vigorous spreading habit, this good all-round fuchsia has fine, very full, double self-pink flowers; the corolla is a little paler than the sepals.

SUNSET (1938)
This cultivar has flowers with small pink tubes, green-tipped sepals and widely flared corollas of glowing coral red – a charming and striking combination. The plant is vigorous and bushy.

Sunset

SWINGTIME (1950)
The double blooms of this popular fuchsia have rich red tubes and sepals and milky white corollas, lightly pink veined. The vigorous growth is erect at first, but droops under the weight of the flowers.

TEMPTATION (1959)
One of the most appealing red and white fuchsias, this single cultivar has each flower with a white tube and slender sepals and a full corolla of orange-rose flushed white at the base. The growth is erect and bushy and flowers profusely.

Swingtime

TENNESSE WALTZ (1950)
Excellent as a standard, but adaptable for all methods of training, this popular cultivar has very full double blooms. Each bloom is formed of a rose-madder tube and up-swept sepals and a charmingly shaggy corolla in a unique shade of lilac-lavender splashed pink.

THALIA (1890)
Although described as a *F.triphylla* hybrid, this delightful cultivar is virtually pure species in form. The slenderly tubular orange-scarlet flowers are carried in drooping terminal clusters, nicely contrasted against the purple-veined, olive-green foliage. With winter warmth it will flower the whole year through.

TING-A-LING (1959)
This is another classic American cultivar of the 1950s which retains its popularity. It is essentially like 'Display' in flower shape and other characteristics, but tube, sepals and corolla are pure white.

TOM THUMB (1850)
A real vintage fuchsia, 'Tom Thumb' remains the best known of a mere

Temptation

Tennessee Waltz

handful of hardy minature cultivars suitable for the rock garden. The small single flowers, in keeping with the size of the plant are produced abundantly over a long season. Each one has a scarlet tube and sepals and a mauve corolla with carmine veins.

TRACE
This pleasing medium-sized double has flowers with cerise tubes and sepals and white corollas with cerise veining. The plant is strong growing and erect.

F.TRIPHYLLA
A native of Haiti and Santo Domingo, this was the first species of fuchsia to be described. Very unlike most popular hybrid cultivars, it is typified by slender tubular, orange-scarlet flowers, bearing very small petals and sepals. These are borne in terminal pendent clusters. The overall effect is very untypical fuchsia, but most decorative. Even the foliage is distinct, each lance-shaped leaf is prominently veined and purple-flushed underneath.

W.P.WOOD (1954)
Compact and fairly slow-growing for a fuchsia, this reliable, hardy cultivar has never gained the popularity it deserves. The somewhat inflated tubes and sepals are scarlet and the purple corolla is stained with the same colour at the base. It makes a striking front of the border plant.

Ting-a-ling

Thalia

Trace

47

INDEX AND ACKNOWLEDGEMENTS

Picture Credits
All pictures courtesy of Gillian Beckett

Artwork Richard Prideaux & Steve Sandilands